# It'll Take Many Days to Explore Russia! The Biggest Country in the World!

## Geography Book for Children
## Children's Travel Books

**BABY PROFESSOR**
EDUCATION KIDS

There is so much to learn about the history of Russia, dating back to 852. In this book, we will be learning about how it came to be the largest country in the world as well as places you might want to visit when you are there and this country's amazing sites to see.

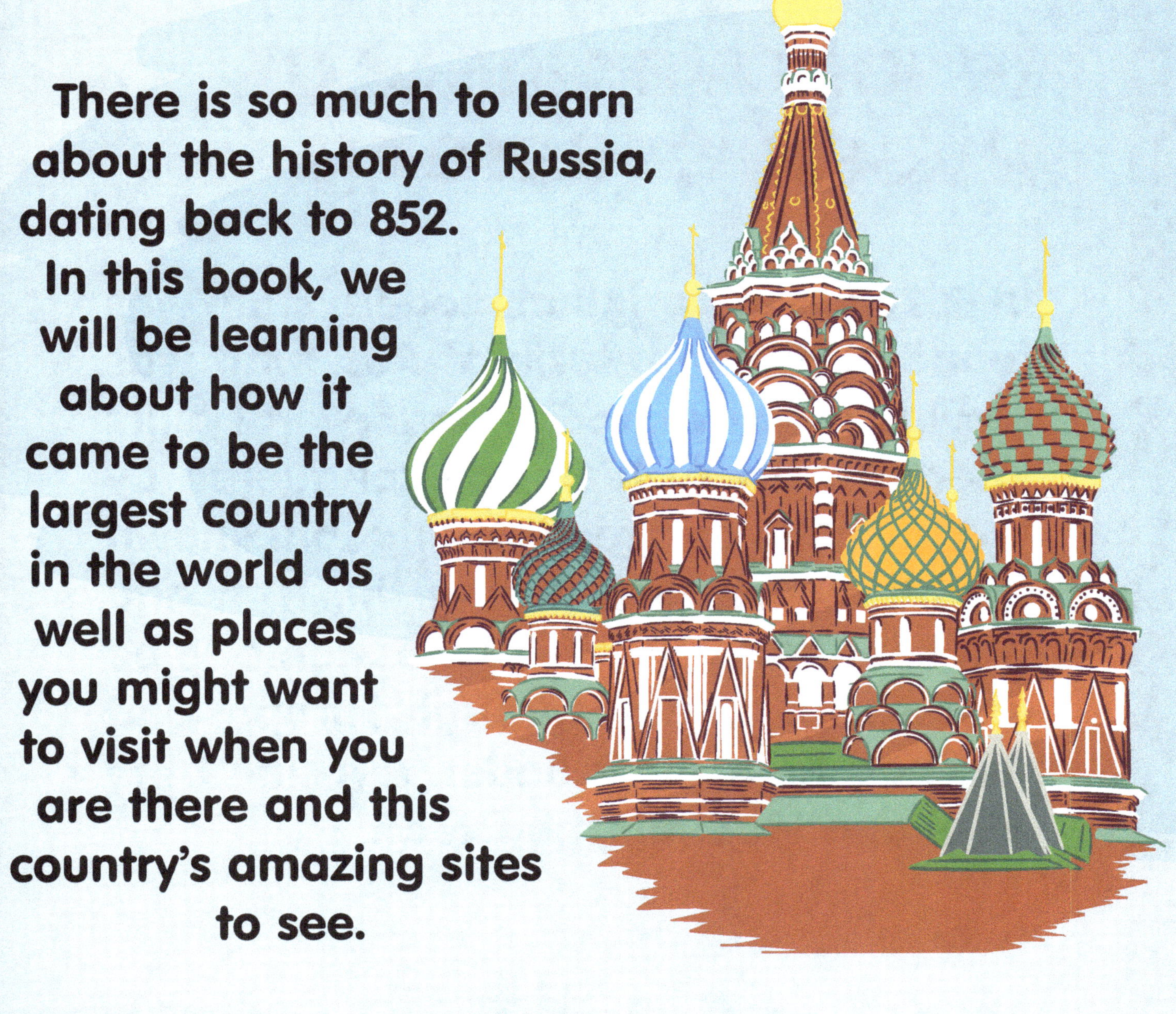

# Brief Overview of Russia's History

In 862, Russia's original modern state was founded by King Rurik of Rus, who was crowned as Novgorod's ruler. Several years later, the city of Kiev was conquered by the Rus, who created the kingdom known as the Kievan Rus. During the 10th and 11th centuries, the Kievan Rus came to be a powerful empire through Europe, and reached their peak under Yaroslav I the Wise and Vladimir the Great.

VLADIMIR THE GREAT

aquesta carauana es partida del
de sarra p̄ anar alcatayo
fusur
iachion
camell
cigicalof
siacui

Led by Batu Khan during the 13th century, the Mongols were able to overtake the area and the Kievan Rus was wiped out.

The Grand Duchy of Moscow saw a rise in power during the 14th century, becoming leader of the Eastern Roman Empire. In 1547, Ivan IV the Terrible proceeded to crown himself as the original Tsar of Russia. Mikhail Romanov founded the Romanov dynasty in 1613, which went on to govern Russia for several years.

VLADIMIR THE GREAT

PETER THE GREAT STATUE IN ST. PETERSBURG

The Russian empire continued its expansion under Tsar Peter the Great's rule from 1689 to 1725, and became an influential power throughout Europe. Peter the Great decided to move the capital of Russian from Moscow to St. Petersburg. Russia culture reached its peak during the 19th century. Famous writers and artists such as Tolstoy, Tchaikovsky, and Dostoyevsky became famous around the world.

In 1917, following World War I, its people fought the leadership of the Tsars. Leading the Bolshevik Party, Vladimir Lenin was able to overthrow this Tsar. In 1918, the civil war started. Lenin's side won the war and in 1922, the communist state known as the Soviet Union was born. After he passed away in 1924, power was taken over by Joseph Stalin. Under Stalin's rule, millions died in executions and famines.

VLADIMIR LENIN

A GROUP OF ORPHANS, SURVIVORS OF THE HOLOCAUST

Initially, Russia became allies with the Germans during World War II. The Germans, however, proceeded to invade Russia in 1941. More than 20 million Russians died during WWII, including more than 2 million Jewish people that were killed as part of what became known as the Holocaust.

FLAG OF THE SOVIET UNION AND RUSSIA

The Soviet Union began developing nuclear weapons in 1949 and an arms race was started between Russia and the United States, in what became known as the Cold War. The economy of the Soviet Union had suffered under isolationism and communism. The Soviet Union collapsed in 1991, and several of its member nations then declared their independence. The area that remained became the country known as Russia.

# Geography

Russia is located on the continent of Asia, and borders the countries of Finland, Norway, Latvia, Estonia, Ukraine, Belarus, Azerbaijan, Georgia, China, Kazakhstan, North Korea, Mongolia, Poland, and Lithuania; as well as maritime borders with the United States and Japan. Its total size is 17, 075,200 sq. km., which is about 1.8 times the size of the United States.

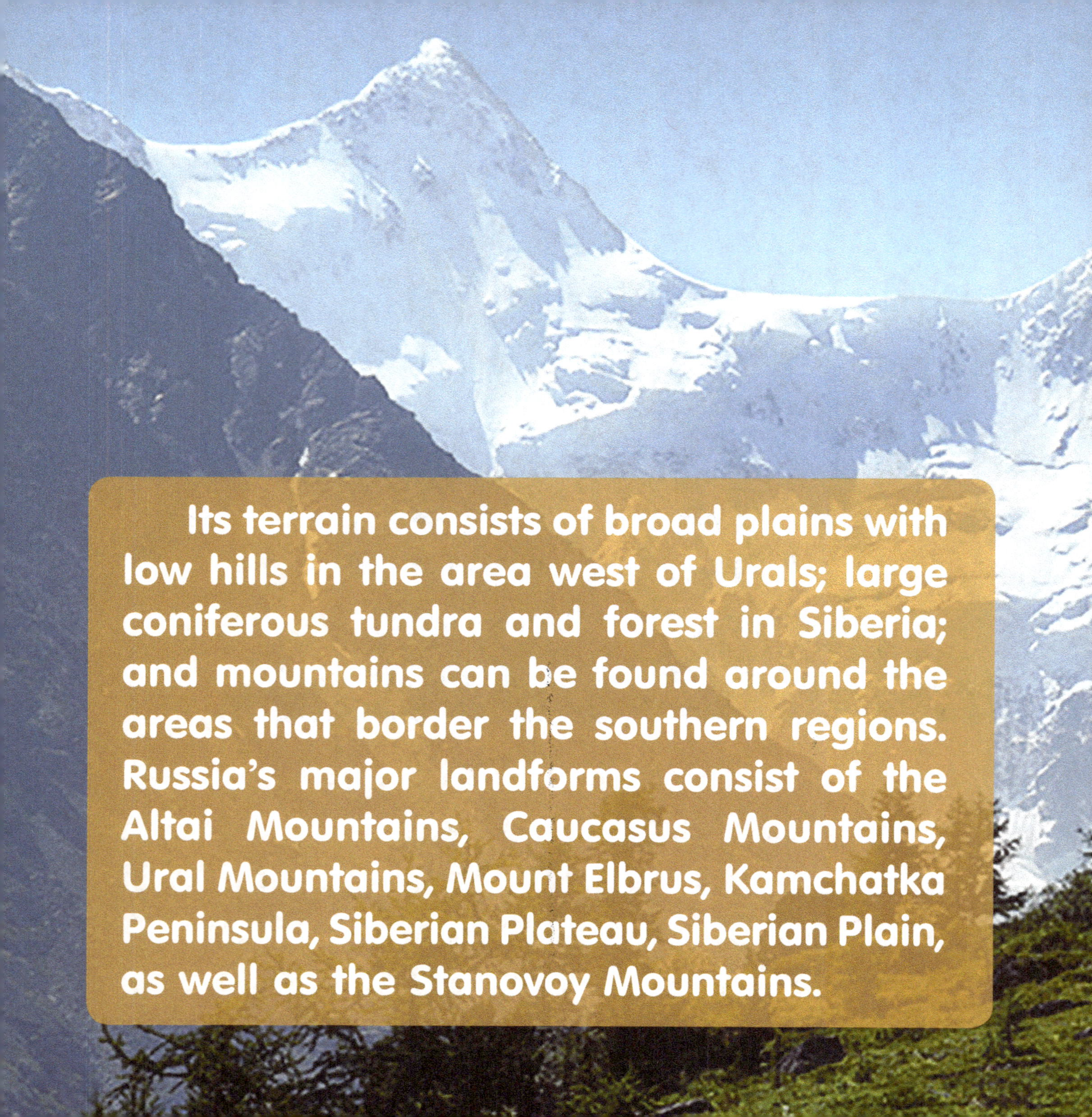

Its terrain consists of broad plains with low hills in the area west of Urals; large coniferous tundra and forest in Siberia; and mountains can be found around the areas that border the southern regions. Russia's major landforms consist of the Altai Mountains, Caucasus Mountains, Ural Mountains, Mount Elbrus, Kamchatka Peninsula, Siberian Plateau, Siberian Plain, as well as the Stanovoy Mountains.

ALTAI MOUNTAIN

VOLGA RIVER

In addition to the Pacific Ocean and the Arctic Ocean, other bodies of water that can be found here are the Ob River, Volga River, Yenisey River, Ladoga Lake, Lake Baikal, Onega Lake, Black Sea, Baltic Sea, Caspian Sea, and the Sea of Azov.

The capital of Russia is Moscow, and other major cities include Saint Petersburg, Novosibirsk, Yekaterinburg, and Nizhniy Novgorod.

RED SQUARE

# Famous Places to Visit in Russia

## Red Square

The history of Red Square is shown in paintings by Konstantin Yuon, Vasily Surikov, and many others. Originally meant to be the main marketplace of Moscow, it also became the site of different public proclamations and ceremonies, and on occasion, they would have the coronation for the Tsars of Russia at the Red Square.

It has been built up gradually since then and has been used by all Russian governments for their official ceremonies.

# Saint Basil's Cathedral

Often referred to as Saint Basil's Cathedral, the Cathedral of Vasily the Blessed, is located at the Red Square in Moscow. Now considered to be a museum, the building is officially the Cathedral of the Intercession of the Most Holy Theotokos on the Moat or the Pokrovsky Cathedral.

Ivan the Terrible ordered that it be built from 1555-61, it memorializes Kazan's and Astrakhan's captures. It was a world-famous landmark and the city's tallest building until the Ivan the Great Bell Tower was completed in 1600.

IVAN THE GREAT BELL TOWER

The Moscow Kremlin

Typically known as the Kremlin, the Moscow Kremlin is a complex that overlooks the Moskva River, Saint Basil's Cathedral, Red Square, and the Alexander Garden. It is the most well-known of the kremlins, including four cathedrals, five palaces, and an enclosing Kremlin Wall containing Kremlin towers. The Grand Kremlin Palace is also located within the complex that serves as the residence of the President of the Russian Federation.

The meaning of the word "Kremlin" is "fortress inside a city", and often is used as a reference to the Russian Federation government similar to how the Executive Office of the President of the United States is referred to as the "White House".

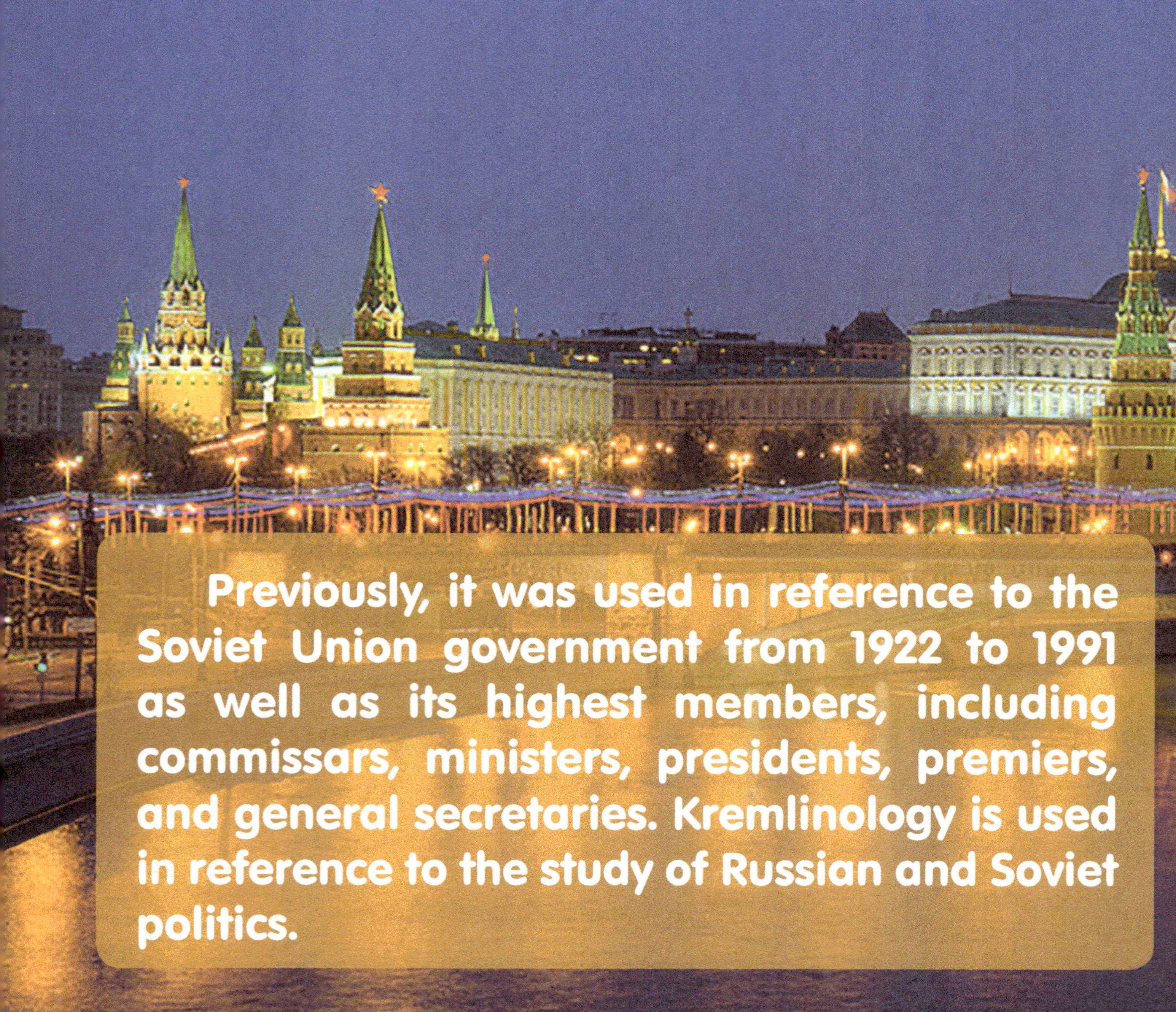

Previously, it was used in reference to the Soviet Union government from 1922 to 1991 as well as its highest members, including commissars, ministers, presidents, premiers, and general secretaries. Kremlinology is used in reference to the study of Russian and Soviet politics.

# The winter palace

Located in Saint Petersburg, the Winter Palace was home to the Russian monarchs from 1732 to 1917. The palace has been restored and now houses the Hermitage Museum. Located between the Palace Square and the Palace Embankment, the fourth and current Winter Palace was constructed between the 1730s and 1837, after it was damaged severely by a fire and rebuilt immediately.

# Mount Elbrus

Mount Elbrus is known as the tallest mountain in Russia as well as Europe, and the tenth highest peak throughout the world. It is a dormant volcano situated in the Caucasus Mountains located in Southern Russia, close to the border of Georgia.

Elbrus consists of two summits, and both are dormant volcanic domes. The west summit is the taller of the two summits at 18,510 feet, or 5,642 metres; and the east summit is 18,442 feet tall, or 5,621 meters. Khillar Khachirov was first to ascent the east summit on July 10, 1829.

MOUNTAINEERS ON MOUNT ELBRUS

In 1874, F. Crauford Grove, leading a British expedition that included Horace Walker, Frederick Gardner, Frederick Gardner, and the Swiss guide Peter Knubel of St. Niklaus climbed the west summit.

Russia is also home to many of the greatest museums around the world, particularly when it comes to visual arts. In Saint Petersburg, the Hermitage Museum is a true star, containing a huge collection first amassed by the wealthy tsars and later by the Red Army and the Soviets. Just as impressive is the magnificent Romanov Dynasty Winter Palace. Often overlooked, the Russian Museum is also a must see since it has the second-best collection of Russian art in the country.

HERMITAGE MUSEUM

VALLEY OF THE GEISERS

# The Natural Wonders of Russia

The natural wonders are worth seeking out if you are a nature lover, even though there are large distances between them. Lake Baikal, located in Siberia, far to the east, is known as its "jewel". Wild Kamchatka, located at the eastern end, almost to Japan and Alaska, is where you will see the Valley of the Geisers, volcanoes, lakes of acid, and bears all over the place.

Located in Russia's extreme south, is the other mountainous territory, known as the Northern Caucasus. This is where you will find Elbrus (discussed earlier in this book), as well as other tall mountains that tower over the Alps. As you travel further east, the landscape becomes more dramatic, from the forested gorges and snow-topped peaks of Chechnya to the desert mountains of Dagestan, which slope down towards the Caspian Sea.

There are more than a hundred Nature Reserves and National Parks to be seen throughout Russia. The Parks are open to the public, and much more undeveloped and wild than you might see in the United States. The Nature Reserves are preserved mostly for research and often are not open to the public.

Certain reserves issue permits, but these are only available through licensed tour operators. However, if you come across the opportunity, you should take it! Kamchatka has some of the more spectacular parks, but the Urals also has some great parks to check out, in particular, at the Altai Mountains.

St Petersburg, Russia

There is so much history and architecture to see, as well as the museums, and the beauty of its land. You will definitely need your walking shoes when you visit Russia, and it may take more than one visit.

For additional information about Russia, you can visit your local library, research the internet, and ask questions of your teachers, family and friends.

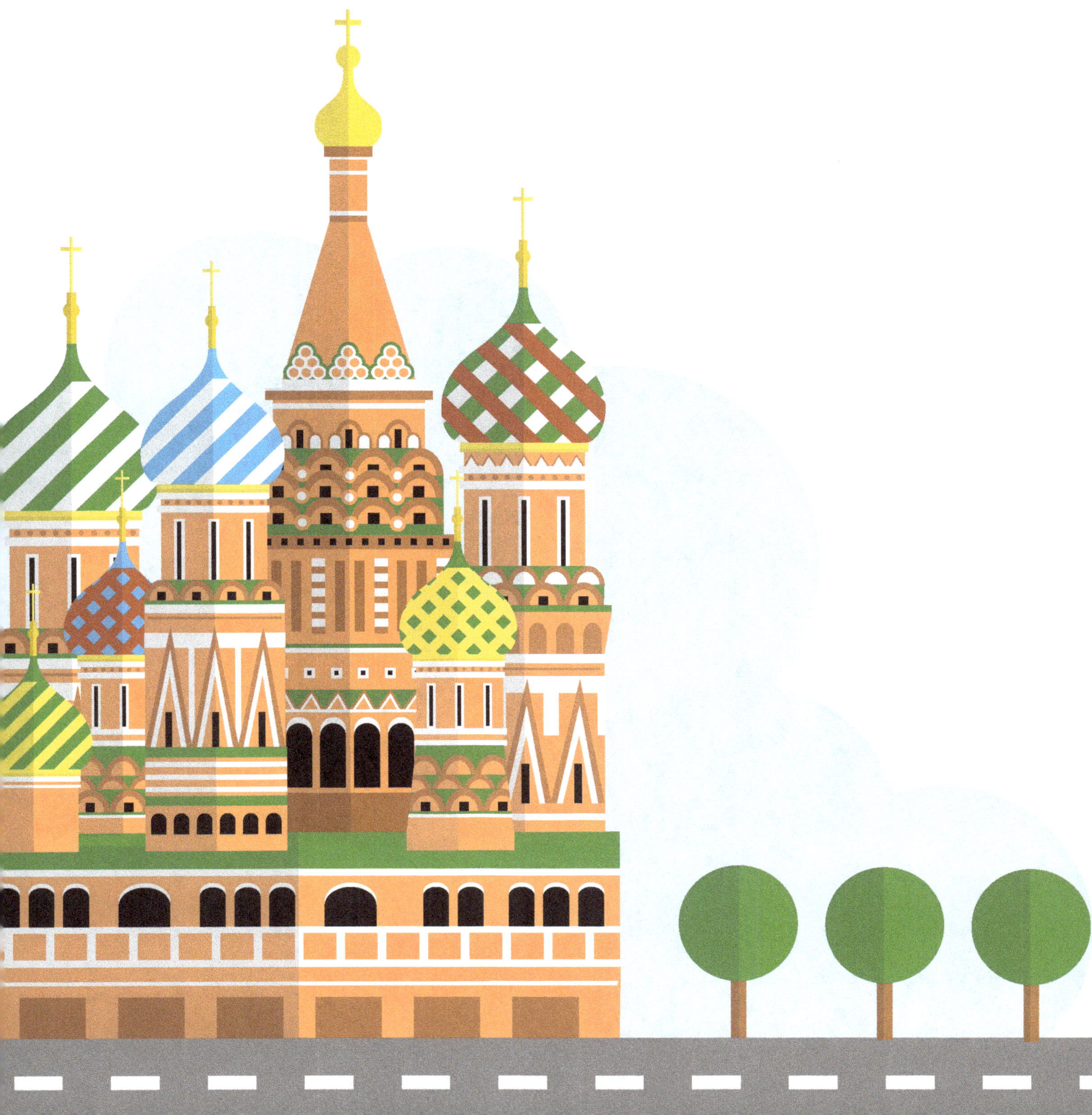

Visit

# www.BabyProfessorBooks.com

to download Free Baby Professor eBooks
and view our catalog of new and exciting
Children's Books